The Oranges
of Revolution

The Oranges of Revolution

Clare Saponia

Smokestack Books
1 Lake Terrace, Grewelthorpe, Ripon HG4 3BU
e-mail: info@smokestack-books.co.uk
www.smokestack-books.co.uk

Text copyright 2015, Clare Saponia, all rights reserved.

ISBN 978-0-9929581-3-8

Smokestack Books is represented
by Inpress Ltd

To Impermanence

'What you're supposed to do when you don't like a thing is change it. If you can't change it, change the way you think about it. Don't complain.'
Maya Angelou

Contents

Foreword 11

Skin
Gerontocrats 15
Constructive thinking 16
second home, second nature 18
London Walls 19
Rash 20
Flatlag 23
Balloon 26
Overdrive 27
Money and the Masturbator 31
Oh shut up and sing me a lullaby 32
Up in Cloud Cuckoo 34
How to kill a living language 35
Playing at Revolution on the Euston Road 37

Pith
Safe Haven 41
Sold to a Cad 42
In your hands – Media Mumbo 44
Curriculum Non Vitae 45
The Staff and Pram 46
Tory Story 49
What's yours is mine. What's mine is mine 50
Terranarchist 52
Patriotism. Protectionism. Paternalism. 53
Demographic Discharge 54
Fish-eye 55
Convenient Intervening 56
Panic 57

Flesh
Ripping livers for libraries	61
I thought you lived in a castle	62
Love priority	63
TLC – Testing on little children	65
Misdirection	67
Tony's Do-it-yourself Guide to the Joy of Revenge	68
Junk-food for Jaws	69
Gadaffi Duck and the looniest of Looney Tunes	70
Butt of the Joke	73
For your own good	74
On a roll	76
A Cable-Car Named (White)House-Fire	77
Tank	79
Short Back and Sides	80
Ironing out Iran	81
Finger-mouse	82
Night Raid	83

Pips
The Face of Revolution	87
No 10 – through the eyes of a ten year old	88
A Daisy Chain called History	90
Debris	92
What is seen	93
I'm all right, Jack	94
Uniform Transparency	96
Joker	97
A fairer (skinned) Constitution – *à la Peste Blonde*	98
Geneva Conventionalism	100
Silent Tourettes	101
Tribe	102
Rheumatic Rebellion	103
Ha(i)ting	105
How to make humans illegal	106
From a Treehouse	108
Crime on Commission	110
For Embolism	111

Illegal Illness	113
A Recipe for Resistance	114
Vocal Accords	116

Juice

In the Cupboard	121
How Social loses sight of Care	122
The Merry-go-round goes round	123
Waste Disposal	125
Apocalyptic Shroud	126
Hotspot at Chilcot	127
Stumped	128
Slapping Stick	129
What we swallow	130
Sublanders	132
Photographic Playground	133
Rewinding	135
Mr. Fixit	137
Free-climber	138
New Dawn	139
Tahrir – Before the Tambourines	14`
Lunchtime Loving in EC2	143
Trading Places	144
Getting Ahead	145

Foreword

The Oranges of Revolution emerged from the hearth of the Arab Spring and explores the knock-on effect subsequently felt around the globe from Cairo to Kiev, not only politically, but also socially, economically and spiritually. The collection is divided into five parts: Skin, Pith, Flesh, Pips and Juice, the consistency of an orange used as a metaphor to depict the various stages of society in its relationship to revolution.

The poems delve into a range of issues belonging to past, present and future, from outdated colonialist values to despotic trigger-happy dictatorships, financial turmoil and social upheaval. They underscore the battle for oil monopoly and the lacking sense of moral responsibility exercised by western powers in a bid to maintain their clout in the market – regardless of human cost. We are living in an age of small-time, imperialist intentions, ex-colonialist nations unable to put down their spears and acknowledge how exploitation and military interference has impacted on the lives of populations both home and abroad. And not to the good. There is no such thing as a *civilising* mission that emanates from hostility, hatred and greed. That in itself is a contradiction in terms.

In any case, we do not need to venture far from base to see the effects of a crumbling system. The collection focuses substantially on the UK's own arthritic social structure as an allegedly developed, democratic and yet increasingly divided nation; the implementation of government policies which favour a rogue banking system and preserve the nation's antiquated class structure, consistently setting the poorest members of society at a permanent disadvantage. The poems explore the causes of the August riots of 2011, the conditions that gave rise to them and how this apparent social meltdown reflects a waning emphasis on basic human values and emotional authenticity at society's core.

The Oranges of Revolution calls to account the coalition's commitment to The Big Society it claims to be moulding, the State's brutally austere budget cuts to vital public services which have ostracised and demeaned the country's most financially fragile, and will continue to affect the nation in myriad ways for generations to come. And yet, despite clear signs of its own social disintegration, the UK still feels duty-bound to persistently impose its supreme ideological wisdom and moral values overseas. This indeed begs the question: what kind of civilised land invests in warfare but cuts welfare?

The collection is intended as an acknowledgement of the global youth's commitment to seeking out an alternative, a distinct, positive echo: there is a choice. It has every right to determine the state of the world it is growing into. The poems were written very much in the spirit of experiencing the moment, my goal being to connect with others from that specific place and mood: to acknowledge convictions, healthy discontent – 'the prelude to progress' in the words of Gandhi – and the pursuit of self-truth. I aim to recognise those who have suffered at the hands of tyrannical regimes; fought and continue to fight for political and social justice around the globe, as well as those who have fallen in the process.

The Oranges of Revolution is not a monologue, cryptic and unreachable. Neither is it about proving a point or claiming to be right. It is about accessibility and human exchange, creating space for real, authentic interactions fundamentally essential in building relationships, advancing the reach of ideas and facilitating change – that ultimately starts from within. After all, what good are words if there's no dialogue?

An orange has segments for a reason: it can be peeled, shared around and digested. It is potential dialogue, not a weapon to be hurled around as a whole – to harm. And with a measure of vision, its pips can be replanted to reap future generations of positive exchange. If we consciously take the trouble to listen to our inner selves: trusting in our intuition and communicating it, instead of passively accepting what is spoon-fed to us via government organs, how much further will society progress? As Leo Tolstoy once wrote: 'Everyone thinks of changing the world, but no one thinks of changing himself.' It requires huge levels of responsibility; looking inside, owning up, choosing how we are seen and heard. But always *choosing*, constantly reassessing what we believe in.

Just a question of trusting ourselves.

Skin

'Never doubt that a small group of thoughtful,
committed citizens can change the world.
Indeed, it is the only thing that ever has.'
Margaret Mead

Gerontocrats

It's the thought before the thought

before the crime

where the noose gets tied
on grounds of telepathy
and the neck of dissent
made out to be anonymous
gets processed, grilled, skinned,

if lucky reformed into an ant
to be stood upon: the treatment
predictable
consistent
unexceptional.

Constructive thinking

There're men now drinking tea
where that house stood yesterday,
toasting to their very own fallen Acropolis
that snaps the Hackney skyline
clean as a chicken's wishbone.
And with nothing to wish on

except a faint carcass of scaffolding
loosely strapped to the neighbouring terraces
like a braid of NHS dentures.

At the foot of the skeleton lies a confetti
of fish 'n' chip boxes
from the kebab house
across the road;

breakfast, lunch and dinner:
the lads plundering their feed
out of cardboard wrappers
before donning the curb
with a token of their efforts.
It isn't every day the dust
of a condemned building
suckles on your eye sockets
when you take your midday trip
to the corner-shop; when you buy
that mammoth newspaper
you'll never read in its entirety
because there aren't enough hours in the day.
For now, the dust descends

across the front page like an unwashed sheep
grazing legs akimbo in the rain. And the front page
becomes the back page; becomes the sky
and scaffolding and rubble;
becomes a cube of nothing
where that house once stood
and an amputation which is still hungry,
greedy and pining for more:
more houses, more fish 'n' chips,
more confetti-kissed sheep
roaming the Hackney patch
between lust and contagion,
waiting for the next.

second home, second nature

second home beyond the walls
of your second
or twenty-second
personality
or that of your brother
or aunt
or fifth cousin
twice removed,

happy for you
to go pussyfooting
around Whitehall;
to have this second home
paid for by those
who haven't even one.

London Walls

It wasn't until they'd strip-searched
the scum surface of ant-trail faeces,
the conveyor belt of instantly ultra-light
satisfactions, the cone-carton-castles
of café practicals, of egg-shell box
polystyrenes; of pink, beige and sage-
green waxed-plastics, smashed and
bashed lovelessly into non-allocated
non-bins

in the wake of weekday exodus

that brick and mortar
exhaled transparency
like a vengeance

they'd never

meant to impose
but couldn't lay to rest.

Rash

I: Symptoms

How long had they said
it was just an incy-wincy
bit of a heat-rash, a mild

implosion

of whinging rose-bud sows
seething like a peel of festering Etnas
from county to county,
cunt to cock,
that should learn
to keep their snouts shut

if only

for the good of their health?

Not a threat, you understand.
Nobody was saying they'd end up
portioned into skin sacks of flabby mutton gut
if they squealed even a muffle of: *'harmer, harmer'*

on the wrong farmer.

II: Denial

If we ply enough make-up on,
who'd ever notice? A cull of porkers
packed down unapologetically
into a mousse of media muteness,
the familiar, sinister trill of ministerial silence,
naming no names beyond the peripheral,
making no admissions without mass coercion,
intravenous intoxication, witch hunt
on an über-national, understated scale:

our colonialist soul is never sick,
never collectively misguided
or wracked with guilt. Never a need
to fess up or assume the worst.
Just burrow and funnel with our arrogance,
all those cowled fears and cloaked tears,
two thousand years of our endemic epidemic
stance; of hooded hoods that should and would

if only they could.

Though they can't –

emotional incompetence chokes eight foot under.

III: Contagion

Water-resistant plasters have lost their grip

in a rain of rampaging boarding masters, caped and tailed
so incapably; head boys looking only for head: an unspoken policy
of stiff upper clit and even stiffer upward-pointing dick
points everywhere and anywhere,

anywhere but at ourselves.

And now how to go back? How to trace and track a mass dispatch
of charismatic waxed Catholics, especially the born again kind;

a perish of parishes

where nobody talks? Nobody bleats. Nobody bites his own lip
while there are other lips to bite. Other nipples to nibble. Other
pansies to pluck. Other infants to muzzle. Battered mothers to fuck;
their babies pre-registered on pre-birth endangered lists –

though clearly no to-do list.

So where do we go?

Social working not in the least bit working.
In fact no one working. Just shirking. Just
an official scrawl like any other to cover
an arse or five. To keep law suits

out of their bathing suits. If they bathe long enough,
who knows, they may even wash away the rash.
And none of it ever happened of course. All treatable
with a flannel of Clearasil.

All squealers to end their days as Savilloys.

Flatlag

It manifests in the form of:
you've gone. You're somewhere

else.

Relocated.
Disorientated.
Sometimes dislocated.

The new patch of land is confusing.
You wake up in Outer Mongolia.
You come home to Istanbul.
In between you've stumbled past a raging pub brawl
on your first night out, six police vans
and a handful of screeching kids
cawing after their arrested fathers
lined up face-down along the nearby side-street
like buckled sardines.

You wonder why you've moved here.
There are sirens scourging every five minutes
and they duplicate through the night
like Gremlins on a binge,
up and down and round the roads;
squad teams of them
keeping watch on the enclosure
from a miniaturised M25, lit blue and red
blue and red
blue and red
blue and red.

The hip-hop howls, marital argy-bargies and Monday night
house-parties have now melted into other sirens, distant sirens
and a slur of Irish bastardisation.

The thirty-story tower block in front of the bedroom
has vanished. In its place is a cowpat of purpose-built,
self-contained pride: brown brick, brown shit. An offshoot
of Strangeways. Three teenagers hang out each afternoon
after school hours in mufti pretending they haven't been
to school, peeved they have no Monday night party
to go to. Not here.

On the other side, lies an orgy of lifeless Victorian terraces
belonging to a colony of ex-hippies and failed artists we never see
beyond the spew of cockeyed, fluorescent drapes
they use to block out the sunlight. Only the couple

directly opposite on the third floor eats dinner.
We spy on them and hazard a guess at what they've made
to require knives and forks, as we sit there with our own provisions
lightly cushioned between fingers and thumb; bread-rolls
that need to be re-hydrated, pan-fried and seasoned
to barely resemble anything even vaguely
stemming from dough. The wooden table
is the plate, the plant-pots: our soup tubs.
And the vase – kindly left by the previous
slob – makes a very fine carafe to drown out
the presence of a somewhat aged Brie
we've tried to bury under numerous layers of linen
like Tutankhamen:

still living, breathing and dying simultaneously.

Though every time the fridge lies agape,
Tutankhamen comes back to haunt
the three remaining rooms of our encasement.
He's greedy. He wants the fridge all to himself.
His own room. His own flat, town and country:
uninhabited, aside from a cluster of serpents
with no sense of pong.

I am no match for Tutankhamen.

He's too strong.
It's too soon.
He's crowding me,
eaten all my space

'til there's more of him than me;

'til the only thing to do is leave the flat.
Leave his flat.
And move

to where Tutankhamen
can't quite run to.

Balloon

How old was I, Dad,

when I first noticed the tone of my skin
barely changed beneath the glare of the sun,

when all the other kids got creams and sprays
and massages every hour on the hour? You passed
me the bottle, exposed your luminous shoulders
that never saw the light of day and expected me
to do the honours. Then, you strapped the longest
whitest bath-towel you could find about your head
and let it drape halfway down your back like an Arabian
Sheikh. You gave me cola and crisps in the shadow
of your parasol: the sand always clustered around the rim
of the can like invisible eggshell. I'd try to spit them
out on the offbeat and you'd tell me I wasn't a camel.

The others all looked like boiled chickens
pointing at the dirt on my freshly bathed torso
that was different to yours and mum's,
Nina and Jack's. I'd try to rub it clean,
the entire body stain stuck to me
like a neurotic polythene bag. I wanted

to know what was underneath. I wanted
to jump up and down on its inflated form
until my insides joined the outside world
and the flaccid shrivel of perished skin
was left trembling in my hand. And

when I come to think about it,
I never really did like balloons.

Overdrive

In my sleep
they took me.

A candle up front
led the abduction

repeatedly
because

it happened every night,
me and a field of Martians
and a canister of Horlicks
travelling at supersonic speeds
between this rave and that,
between cannons, deserts, typhoons,
weddings, funerals, births, prostate
cancer operations, bungee jumps,
UN conferences, HM prison riots;

between business-class, trans-world crossings
on United Arab Emirates and caravans standing for
emergency health service sanctuaries
in all privileged US townships.

I tank up on soya beans and GM-free algae. I get high
with the others on rapeseed oil and maize shakes.
I am a Martian – I am happy to say and my last mission
took me to William Hill on the Kentish Town Road,
Halloween 20-17: I got drunk – very drunk – on stale algae wine,
lost all senses and made a bet 5093 to 1 that aliens would come
to the Kentish Town Road that night.

I promised to take snaps.

The guy behind the till rolled his eyes double-time
towards the customer to his left, towards his colleagues
dotted about the shop floor, raising their brows
to a whisper of: 'got a right one 'ere, mate!'

But he let the bet go through. Something like doubt
or the sweet scent of victory he couldn't quite resist,
eyes all the while rolling like washing machines.
I got giddy and keeled over. The owner screamed
when my mask didn't come off.

I confess I'm a gambler.
I can gravitate.
I can levitate.
I can contaminate
both lawfully and unauthorised.
I'm a party and can copulate over Copacabana

if I want.

I don't need to be tolerant or pragmatic.
I don't need to consult anyone.
I can turn my flesh inside out.
When I blush against the skyline on an open sea
I become a Dali painting. I am fantasy.
I'm a bet only I will win.
I suck on your bone marrow for antibodies,
top up on blood like an Oyster card,
checking in and out of humanity
when it suits. When it bores me.
A day amongst people is a long time.

I've made a film about this:
bring fossils back to life
unlike David Attenborough
and dance in their footprints
'til the globe has flattened out again,
pain: anaesthetic, often adrenalin,

the world at night that sleeps
when there's so much to be done.
I get into vaccines, the diarrhoea
of a Typhus colony. I can leap
between Mexico and Malawi
at the poke of a belly button.

I have telescopes from my fingertips and the world
is my opera house; one sick, empty crime thriller after another
with the odd bit of lurrrvve thrown in for good measure. I
watch

the murders and rapes, the pandemics
seeping through from continent to continent
like butter on hot crumpets. They call it flu
because it defies flight, transcends time zones,
mechanical and medical intelligence. They are
the aliens that already inhabit the Earth,
that mate with infants
and then smash their heads on asteroids
to put them out of their misery.

They too make bets from their observations
and always win. I watch multi-faceted corruption
scams, backhanders behind politicians' doors,
swapping snuff for silence,

for uranium,

for rare, unheard-of antidotes. I watch

the lies jotted down in order of cost,
sealed and packed away from the public
in corrugated iron safes. I watch the whispers

I cannot decipher but understand.
I pass on this understanding. This hunch. The whiff
of deception you have a right to know and rebuff.

I am always on standby, always networking
and growing relative to your crimes. Displaced.
Deployed: I volunteer for the lot. The world
is a billboard of cork and I press drawing pins
into it like a diseased voodoo doll
waiting to be healed,

her medicines cascading in lists,
categories,
columns,
grids,
bar- and pie-charts;
Information, information,
databases,
monitors with capricious temperaments, reflections
of poor understaffed customer service, poor
communication, infrastructure outsourced
to the wrong people; the answers
they don't know are answers.
They don't know.
They don't ask questions.
Just make more errors.
Transmit more disease.
More terror.

They say too much.
And now my memory is full
so I can't help them.

I just want to sleep.

Money and the Masturbator

Money likes to go to fancy-dress parties, done up to the nines
in anything from computer hardware to the latest Louis Vuitton
handbag. He goes nowhere without a top-of-the-range Ipod,
Iphone and iconic identity crisis screwed into his head – beside
his credit card details

naturally. Money has difficulty communicating effectively
without the aid of some externally attached apparatus shielding
his sensibilities. He trolls about the city's streets by night
strutting his stuff. He thrives on a wee dram of prostitution
and often reproduces because of it.

He says he's just exchanging favours.
He says everyone's a slag at heart.

Money likes both girls and boys though: any age, any species.
His most favourite fancy dress costume, of course, is a dollar-bill
suit he bought to mask his sexual inadequacies. He can wear this
whenever he wants because he has power and people will do
anything to pull him. Own him. Breed him. Ensure his survival.

Money is sex enshrouded in a full-length barbed cape. He likes
to peep out from behind his disguise once in a while by way of
foreplay. Because Money loves to play.

Pretend.
Hide.

And seek. 'Cause he's always on the game, is Money.
Always selling his soul for some whim or other,

and missing the point.

Oh shut up and sing me a lullaby

It wouldn't have been quite the same
learning to talk

without that ubiquitous hole
in our warped terraced fencing
through which Simon blitzed his first words
age four, much to the pride
of his three older brothers
and the pre-pubescent wisdoms they'd imported
from the Grange Hill school of niceties.

Some said that Mr. Peterson, the septuagenarian
neighbour, with a natural aptitude for Victor Meldrew enactments,
had had it coming to him, having slashed the boys' third
and only remaining football
that afternoon –

and clearly without remorse.
Not surprisingly, it wasn't *mama* or *dada*
burning to greet Simon's virgin lips, but
'Oy, Mr. P, fuck off!'

Mr. Peterson, now thoroughly outraged
at the impertinence, thrust his foot at the space
where Simon's four year-old smirking gob had been
but achieved no more than consecrating his right boot
to the bunch of hooligans next-door. He knew
they would fill it with water – or worse – as they'd done
the last time, and that their parents would utter
the same worn-out excuse yet again to exonerate them:
'well, boys will be boys, Frank.'

Well, Frank wanted to tell Kath and Don
where to stick their boys. He hopped
up and down like a rabid bull-frog,
hollering every expletive under the sun
and swelling redder to mauver
until he closely resembled something
of an unappeased erection
with a fisherman's cap on top:

all from a kid who was potentially dumb, and now,
suddenly on the verge of quoting Nietzsche.

The boys patted themselves on the back,
hi-fived in Mexican waves
and rolled about on the lawn in hysterics
at the sight of Mr. Peterson's terrorised facial expression,
his upper torso half impaled on the beginnings
of an unkempt pyracantha he'd never meant to care for – but did
because it deterred the little blighters
from climbing onto his turf.

Kath and Don delighted at Simon's newfound eloquence.
He was a regular memory bank and found himself
twenty years later steeped in artificial intelligence. It was
like having a parrot for a child. Never knowing
what would go in, and more to the point,
what might come out. There was no telling how MI5
would have faired had Simon been cooing his way
through a series of illegal warfare breastfeeds;
how chilly Chilcot might have turned out,
caught short in a swing of toddling seniority

that claimed more than gardening boots
from some sour old git.

Up in Cloud Cuckoo

The remains of his reign rearrange themselves
like spoilt split tuna flakes indecently undressed:
raw, butt-naked, dethroned director who's failed
to master his mise en scene, tripping from Tripoli
to miserable Misrata on a death-wish. He sides

with mismanagement, a deployment of diplomats
who've lost more than just the plot. They'll
condone crackdowns and butchery and prime-time
TV castigations; cross-border crossings that
become mirages to his own coveted tread. 'Cause

up in Cloud Cuckoo and away with the fairies he flies,
both time and blood sewn seamlessly to each eye,
the years in those tears that his citizens cry, the hours
and minutes lost to his lies, and the rhyme in this despot
who's known nothing but crime: Not fine. Not alright.

Stop.

How to kill a living language

Arms crossed,
legs crossed,
lips, ribs, fingers, lungs crossed;
tongues tied or crossed,
or whipped, stripped
and yanked out,
vocal cords deconstructed
or rewired
to a silent hint of vegetation,

otherwise known as respect.

Why are we here?
Why are you here?
This isn't French.
It's meditation: you're
doing nothing more
than detain us en silence;
nothing in any language.

When you say *entrez*,
it's like entering a monks' retreat
with the enlightenment bit taken out.
And you'd prefer we said nothing
than hollered across the room
in perfect French. You ban
all forms of mouth rotation
from speech to chewing gum
to learning, and back again.
And you know you're
the only chance we have

to get off this island. You've exported
bezazz from the curriculum. You
can make or break our interest,
sully our ambitions, make us develop
a lifelong aversion
to everyone of your landsmen.

But you don't care

just as long as long as you get
your fifty minutes of tranquillité,
we can despise who we want – later on.
Our ignorance is a small price to pay:

irrelevant that we've learnt zilch,
that we've been here five years
and still can't introduce ourselves
or open the textbook to the right page

because we can't even count from one to ten
in your tongue; you've divided it into wafer-thin slivers

of impossibility. Because you run your lessons
like the Fifth Amendment, with no-one defending
our right to speak,

our right to learn.

We've warmed our boots on your fire
and you've turned up the flames
and stamped on us.

You'd rather we were silent. Or absent.
You'd rather we'd chosen Spanish.
But you have to pay your mortgage somehow.

Playing at Revolution on the Euston Road

Take it or leave it. Book-shelf-borrowed.
CND-trained. Carbon copy of National-
Archive resource let off the leash: flyers
promising a fight to the death but sent
with only half a heart on dummy-runs
past puffy street constables and over-
curious CCTV footage that doesn't know
what it's looking for.

Faking membership in the name of
mass murder and martyrdom. Martians
landing on the other end of Eden
like a misfire of sub missiles. The
signpost indicated the south-side
of Camden Town. A larynx of
delinquent harps running amok
in my head. The tripping rustle

of undressed sweet wrappers and
scrapped pencil shavings. Found
no fame in academic madness,
a vow of silence deliberated some-
where between time and apocalypse.
We access disgust. We polish the
word, spread it and forget to breathe.
We are peers in waiting. And we'd go

outside, if we could.

Pith

'Education is the most powerful weapon
which you can use to change the world.'
Nelson Mandela

Safe Haven

Come. Invest. Share.
Shed your billion dollar bills
here and there. Keep our
delicate delinquent universities
afloat. 'Cause our own government
sure as hell can't.

We'll forget your past
if you forget our present
(state of demise), take a load off our taxpayers,
our teenagers; trade as many arms
and legs

as you like
just as long as they remain
on your side of the Sahara.

Did you know scruples was a made-up word
intended for miming parties and masquerade balls? That
stability was the lovechild of revolution? That instability
was a leader rocking his regime to sleep, hydrophobic bear
and a treeful of nestlings jiving fifty-two to the dozen?
And we'll feast while they starve, on lamb shanks
and chicken bellies, on stealth and sanctimony.
We'll demand no-fly zones but fail to mention
those bloody-minded mosquitoes loitering
with oil-barrels and credit card in the wings
and always,
always

smelling something in the pipeline,
waiting for the lights
to go out.

Sold to a Cad

In memory of Cadbury's of Bournville

It was as though a mangle of bulbous lemons
were gyrating to the swell of her conscience
as she cast her glance out to sea, a squint
long and sterile protruding from the left iris
like a monolithic shrine

attacked by plague, tricked by an enchanting hunger
that vainly mirrored the roar of beggars
from three thousand miles off. Each:

a violet silhouette taming the next,
'til the waves became a sheath of purple thugs
chanting BURY THE CAD. BURY THE CAD.
Pimping the great chocolate prostitute in all her finery,
until she's up the spout from a hybrid-lactose incubus
that may never make the crossing; that may never hatch
from a mother-hen who now breeds congealed cheese
for a living

easily mistaken for toothpaste
were she not nesting but two feet away from Monsieur
Roquefort, Camembert, Dolcelata, and crew.

A simple oversight.
An even simpler Apartheid

for consumers kept illiterate on dairy-style dental products
boasting less milk than Bournville. Though this mother-hen

hasn't brushed for years. From now on, she'll eat chocolate
cheesecake for every meal, be the walking, talking migraine
to jumpstart the nation every morning, the model denture
patient with more fillings than enamel.
And still she smiles.

Even when there's no cure vast enough
to fill the lost belly of a land; a middle England
that's molten to a hollow, snow to a stove,

a soup of squeezy cheese
that can't even remember
when it left an udder –
IF it ever left an udder
or a cactus
or any excretory orifice
even vaguely resembling
sparrow sphincter valves

before ending up black sheep of the dairy counter,
crafty impostor of the cocoa aisle, whore of the month
in your new suit of metallic mauve; you drop your pants
at every opportunity, anticipation empty as a wooden chair
with the backside carved out. For

when you fall between,
or when you're caught
or held or hugged
or shown that hot August handbag
just a wee bit too long,
you find you dice with nature:
drip through those
cheesy
purple
drawers.

In your hands – Media Mumbo

By force, of course
it happened two weeks after it did,
camera frozen on a wing of devotion,
flossing the crowd with less than
approximate vulgarity for that nice, neat slice
it wants to speak for. The rest

is a plague of pummelled custard tarts.
Everywhere, the elaborate trim of
indulgence embalms,
mashed-up Middle East
as a feast. More than just the smile
you wish to capture: bristles, glasses,
female moustaches; cheeks steeped
in revolution's grime, soiled for weeks.
Unrecorded. Unregistered. No patience

for that kind of truth.

Because everyone loves a good film
and you have all the tools: Hollywood to die for.
Though you prefer to call it documentation,
current affairs. A serious profession. One
built on conviction, a pang of personal
responsibility to call injustice to account.
Nothing to do with the fact it pays your bills,
your three mortgages, keeps you in funds, in favour
with the Foreign Office. Ludicrous times crown you
the hero, serenading the globe's news-junky
gaggle from a glass tower so fragile

your own arias stand to shatter procedure.
Not your solo, darling. Not your party.

Curriculum Non Vitae

The child whose face lights up at a kid-dult film,
but is lost behind curriculum, leaves, tundra,
expectation;

foul demands that point fingers and taunt
illiterate bitch! She strips them bare.
She becomes an ASBO wannabe

for the day.

Can she spell?
Can she count?
How many times

has she been to the magistrates
and back since the age of twelve?
Though she has views:

she went through the plot
and characters
with a fine-tooth comb.

She said they painted the truth;
the one she would have told
had she been able to spell

the fight
she clamours
in a sulk. And I know

YOU are not indifferent.
Because you said
you liked reality.

The Staff and Pram

Roll up! Roll up!
for the staff and pram:
knights on white bicycles
with shining IPhones
for swords
and a terrine of Pitbulls
for shields, scrawny,
lanky wimps playing papa
for a laugh: this is the face
of your British Empire –

shaven scalps and stickle-bricks
head-locked hound to hound
with another platoon
of ready-to-kill staffs
fresh from the SAS nightschool
of nextdoor's neighbouring estate.

Their gals jangle gold
from extremities that shouldn't
make public appearances,
a flamboyant offering of stretch marks
amongst other loose bits
setting themselves free.
They're under half my age
and comparing their babies' Nike trainers
down the Costcutter,
donning a pram
like the latest space-age craze
of make-up accessories.
Babe on wheels.

They swap Top Trump cards
and scrap over those lost.
Kid without an earring
is minus-twenty

on the cool scale. Gold hoop
rammed through the lobe
once
maybe twice
with a pit-bull canine,
kebab skewer, nana's
knitting needles used to tag
like a honing pigeon
brought to assembly: the Jets
and the Sharks and the whole
dammed Westside buggy brigade.
Stand to attention.

As if there were a GCSE in that:

text books and history scripts
not worth the paper they're written on,
slapped by foundation and lipstick,
hair-gel and hand-creams. 'Wha d'ya
mean, Miss?' they yawn again,
licking mascara onto their lashes,
the clues remaining locked, daunting,
tauntingly cryptic. She means to
pull out a highlighter

but falls upon a fag-lighter, lip
and eye-liner, the safe familiarity
of their feel. Their submission.
Their flattery. No questions asked.
No demands. No failure. Just pretends
she lives in the world of Make-Face-
Book, the Willy-Wonker-land of gossip
and insincerities; unfed spider's web
where the Russian Revolution
and William Wordsworth are captured,
beaten, swallowed down and spat out
whole. The Guantanamo of knowledge.
Duck out of the way of possibility. Paint
over it in a mask of emulsion she's used
to banish lines, features, character,
individuality, personality. She becomes
the make-up. Becomes the almond-soot
rings about her eyes, the glistening jelly
of her lips, the drooling blue hearts
and names and arrows scrawled across
her limbs, her once bony shoulder blades,
the cavern beneath her already sloppy breasts,
a map of where she's been

and who she's forgotten;
where she'd wanted to go, the child
within lost to redraftings, crossings-out,
recycled booby traps: children protruding
from the ground as half stumps, education
the fading provision offering no appeal
other than charity.

Tory Story

Books
not bankers
not bonkers
not bonuses. They
strike a match
and set a light
to the lot in salty
stolen bonfires,
someone else's
story. Toy story.
Tory Story.

They've acquired
a taste for them
like stuffed black
olives and dry-
roasted cashews
and crabmeat
and caviar

on brown toast.
They evacuate
the stones

with a projectile
gobbing motion
and watch them
land piecemeal
indiscriminately
two-at-a-time;
pregnant Sparrow
missiles that cannot
self-destruct.

What's yours is mine. What's mine is mine

It wasn't where he'd wanted his money to go
when he said yes to that night-job, manoeuvring
himself around terraced desk arrangements
with a feather duster

at Brigg's Call Centre, Dudley, Birmingham.

Clive got £5.90 an hour
for pretending not to see the deposits of smack-stashes
lining the underskirt of every third chair, beer-cans
in every other filing cabinet between the invoices
marked *resolved*; backlog copies of *FHM*
lurking beneath each and every list
of who to call and pester first thing tomorrow.
And to think, he made the office
such a pleasant, clean place to be,

his clean wages providing clean taxes
to buy comparatively unclean second homes
for those happily declaring: Fuck jobseekers!
Arbeit macht frei! For those sending a quarter
of his pittance to a polarised poppy-farming fraternity
way out yonder, sovereigns of insurgency,

sovereigns of urgency
now that the Milky Bar Kid's switched
to that light fluffy stuff and boasts: Opium's on me –

but don't expect me to suck you off.

Now Clive's worldliness didn't go much beyond
the front page of the daily rag he chucked away
should his mind wander away from the hash'n'
smack stashes tucked up in his confidence.

Clive was confused.

He thought Helmand Province was where
the mayo for his ham butties came from.
He thought Kandahar was that French football player
who spoke with a *told* in the nose, and Peshawar
what he dunked,

rhythmically, of course,

in his Balti every Friday
after one too many down the local.
He said he'd always liked Peshawar.

It didn't occur that the white fluffy stuff
might come from the same place
as his mayonnaise or that
the backlog copies of *FHM*
might be sent via Christian Aid
in the name of Fucking Human Misery.
At least with Jobseekers', the taxes
had gone to him

and not to nuclear this, or WMD that,
not accidentally lost to warlords, Ex-but-not-inactive-Ex-PMs
merrily playing peacekeeper and breeding poppies, poppies,
poppies for Briggs' intercultural smack habit.

So much responsibility on Clive's shoulders
for that £5.90 an hour. But he soon shoehorned
the thought back to its rightful home – and turned

to page three. Perhaps he'd ask for a pay-rise.

Terranarchist

Love thy neighbour. Well bollocks to that:
Love thy STASI-esque-state even more
and tell us about your neighbour, best buddy,
all those beastly family members
you could never stand anyway. Tell us

about their stateless faith, their latest trip
to the polling booth; how many times
they've spoken of trashing Fortnum and
Masons in the past year. Because they're

as noxious as they are obnoxious,
curiously foul, verminous, infectious,
morbiferous, pestilential, fatally septic
and lawless beings who should be
wiped of the right to free expression

care of Democracy.

Tell us in time for Christmas
and you'll receive a once-in-a-lifetime
Big-Cash reward from your cousin Conner,
tax rebate on the first £9440 of your earnings,
not to mention 10 extra free-of-charge Tory-
stamped, vetted and validated electoral
roll-cards. Guaranteed to make you talk
of the town. That is, if the Terranarchists
don't get you first.

(For definition of Terranarchist, please consult
the latest revised version of Death Chamber's
English Dictionary.)

Patriotism. Protectionism. Paternalism.

She takes on board centuries
of pre-revolutionary legends.
She steals into their rhythms
and un-thought-out stipulations
of ignorance. She relies on a
perpetuated lack of clarity, cloaks
of suspicion, wreaths of jealousy.
She incubates the fears of healthy
newborns. She grows some more
in test-tubes and turns a blind eye
to their effervescence.

You might mistake her for being
a vacant racist but really she's
just imbecilic, extracting every
ounce of momentum from the

movement

amongst a dirge of martyrs
summoning Joan of Arse.

Demographic Discharge

Just bump 'em off
if they're old enough:

that's what the small print reads
between the sheets, paying carers

less for longer like steam-rolled
Andrex puppies. Crisis is a self-made bed,

made but once a year out of burnt hay
and brittle twig-sticks. Decay creeps in

at snail speeds. Decay parties after hours,
too thick-skinned to leave. The Tory big-pig heart

keeps'em all far from the TV screen;
keeps'em or kicks'em out of clinic

and home and hospital beds on the grounds of
insubstantial evidence. Though,

in the discharge papers it says
as you exit through the door,

pounds, shillings and pence
could have changed all that

were you *To the Manor Osborne*.
But you're not. Obviously. And how many

actually are? Just listening for their knell.
Geriatricide in slow motion.

Fish-eye

Windows on the world
but no doors. I asked for
a fishing net and cricket
bat and spin-bowled into
what looked like a letter
box – at first sight.

It turned out to be plate glass.

It shattered.

It shattered with a garish,
fish-scented sunset,
submerged in a bay rinse
of trash and starvation.

There were pin-striped lives
tumbling out of tall buildings
ablaze with youth's defeated
speak, shut out behind foot-
thick vaults and cast-iron
safety gates like infectious
cancers trying to speed-date
in the dark – and with no more
than an eye socket

between them.

But no glass.
And no windows.
And barely a world.

Convenient Intervening

Because it suits
and a trial costs
more than money
more than time
and manpower
hours, more than
taxpayer consent

and media consultation –

Because of the rush
for all that rushes
stampedes ahead
of sense

and judgement
and moral grounding

and because the truth
has got its tongue
tied up in pathological
rhetoric and lost its
meaning

to the convenient.

Panic

The only thing left on the street
was horseshit arranged in bulky
little lots the length of the city.

You could tell where they'd been
whipped and boot-clenched,

the horses, that is,

then further on where they'd
bolted and moulted and left piece-
meal souvenirs of human-induced
paranoia

for the taxpayer to mop up.

Flesh

'If you want to have a lie worth living,
a life that expresses your deepest feelings and emotions
and cares and dreams, you have to fight for it.'
Alice Walker

Ripping livers for libraries

Why don't they join the liver trade?
Just in time for Christmas. 10 000
lots of offal far from plan and proportion
would tighten the belt on the bill;

would shape the face of loan and ransom.

If they joined the liver trade, they could
lobotomise laboratories for free, donate
a haggle of tax concessions
to the likes of Topslob
and Voodoophone
and set research to rest.

Except in defence.

'Cause the big cheese likes liver.
Especially teenage ones. He gets fat
on the fois gras of undergraduate mishap: undercutting,
underfeeding, under-educating, underkeeping
the unkempt kingdom of the UK you might
be tempted to rechristen the YUK.

So death to academia –

between Google and the government,
literature doesn't really stand a chance:
ripped and RIP-ed and sold down the river
with ransom notes in hand. For some

bodies are priceless, irreplaceable
and cannot reincarnate.

I thought you lived in a castle

It wasn't just the way in which you said
you lived on the twelfth floor

as if you owned a castle: in Deptford,

the thin soles of those canvas slip-ons
four sizes too big, second or fifth or thirty-fifth
hand and rusted about the buckles, that cotton coat
with not even mesh for lining, those gloveless fingers
and wool tights with more holes than wool; that breakfastless
vomit you showed me. You showed me your stomach
has another purpose you don't understand. You say

mother told you that.

In those canvas shoes, you spin around
all beads and dreads. You bounce higher
on that empty stomach than the others.
And then you nod off. Suddenly. Sat up.
With those others. All of you in that cycle:
freshness. Exhaustion. Hunger. Excitement.
Luck. Poverty. Love. Abandonment. Attention-
seeking. I understand why and when you do it.
I don't want to turn you away too.
The power is not mine. It rings

like a telephone when it wants; at four,
your distraction isn't linked to the financial state
of you. At eleven it is. At fifteen, criminality welcomes.
At eighteen, they talk of inevitability.

They didn't know you at four.
You were untouchable. Not broken.

Love priority

How? It's forgotten so quickly; wham, smash,
the lions and tigers and pregnant paparazzi
all fed out of the same genetically modified trough:
five weeks of Tsunami saga and nuclear news havoc,
the worst disaster since Chernobyl, since World War II;

since any point in history where nature and man
have crossed swords and fucked each other off.
And suddenly, Japan does not exist: one man's
conspired execution supersedes that of 30 000
natural ones. So now the truth is out. Nobody
really cared in the first place. Just another

fleeting glance at doom and gloom jazzed up
through the monocle of morning media sharks;
jack off the latest TV-rated-sensation with neither
further heed nor sympathetic inclination. 'Cause
sympathy dines only with obese sales stats. He
likes'em curvy, well-rounded

up

before copulating. When they fail to reproduce
he dumps them. He adheres to the belief:
sluts aren't for life. Just for Christmas. They

determine what we read and perceive, what we
avoid, ignore and forget, what we feel and digest;
confused, lounging, ever hopeful in front of weddings
that are not our own. Even the gym shows 3 screens
of white dress out of 4. The fourth is snooker. This
is supposed to motivate. How the hell do you run 5K
on that? The long shots send me hurling off the side
of the travellator. But this is the news. World affairs
are reduced to a white dress and chalky waistcoats
wafting round Westminster. Japan ok today.

Tomorrow too, when honeymoon-hustlers get their way.
The day after, the binning of Bin Laden rules the waves.
In a week's time, something else. Tragedy lost as quickly
as it came, now stocked up with bright copper wigs and
magnetic tweezers. Forgotten. Never happened. Not royal

enough. Long gone and so terribly dull.

Terrorist chainsaw massacre – not dull. For example.
Press obsession with terrorist successor almost as
impressive as the terrorist's obsession with terrorism.
But Japan unnamed. So Japan ok. Japan shrinking,
diminishing, floating downstream; all the red rays on its
verdant flag turning pink from the melt – but Japan ok.
Japan ok. All silenced on the Eastern Front.

TLC – Testing on little children

Running out of cures for this and that,
the dead soon become fossils too
to be poked around
for the twenty-sixth
thirty-ninth
forty-seventh time. By the sixtieth

they give up the ghost; outstretched
moat peels back off the dissecting
table: rusty, bubbled and singed about
the edges like an oven-crisped pizza

top.

The animals said they weren't too keen
on internet testing either: the e-pigs
complained of repetitive strain injury
from being rammed back and forth
through the hard drive. The e-rats
regretted a permanent state of epilepsy
from being tin-packed behind the
monitor screen. Whilst the e-chimps
had become fatally addicted to Apebook,
Banana Fritter and Yahoo-hoo-hoo.

Free love was reported to have hit
an all-time low, as had Swinger Club
and Shag & Carry loyalty cards.

It seemed the e-animals were simply
not coming up with the goods.
Nothing new. Nothing new.
ICI-aye-capt'n losing its welly.
Pfizer, its soul.

The chief neurologist scratched her head.
The chief pharmacist picked at his scalp.
They eyed each other slyly, the spotlight
of skin-shavings they were stamping around in,
before cagily turning their attentions towards
the two hundred children playing football
beyond the fence-trim

with an out-of-date dialysis bag.

Who would even notice?

As long as there was milk and maize
and medicine enough to haul them in
by the cartload. Just this once

while the pigs made the most of maternity
leave, the rats taking to the couch
quack in hand, and the chimps, by now
almost asexual, underwent the town's
most prestigious fertility reawakening
programme: Oestrus all over.

Just this once
while business was bad
because there are medicines to be made
and bills to be paid. And if we can't invent
new drugs,

we'll just have to invent new disease.

Misdirection

There are

more factions
fighting factions,
than factions

fighting for freedom, competing

for how many bystanders
they can massacre,
collecting bodies

like marbles. If

you roll a marble
off the edge
of the earth,

when will it stop rolling?

Weapons and cash
are bartered for loyalty.
Will and desire

and patriotism

cooked up long ago
in a hearty tub of lard fat.
Though now the dripping

has gone to the dogs, old

and mouldy.

Tony's Do-it-yourself Guide to the Joy of Revenge

Revenge has such silent paws.
He leaves his spots on the bathroom cabinet
of a morning so as not to weight him down

like his appetite. He buys fresh flesh
every Friday from the local warmonger
after pretending not to listen to Woman's Hour.
He follows a rigid regime: accountability for breakfast.
Blame for lunch. And a hearty portion of denial for dinner –
as part of a well-balanced diet. He wanks off
whenever Murray's voice dives an octave.

Revenge is scrupulously clean. He bathes
in belligerence more than five times a day.
…Well, he has to try to scrub all the blood-crud
beneath his nails… Not his own. Naturally.
And *Vanish* never worked.

But most of all, Revenge likes to sleep: can't function
without a fully fluffed-out eight hours since he also likes
to wake at the crack of dawn and spring surprise visits
on his unsuspecting neighbours. His favourite possession
being a 20 year-old manual Lorus Quartz alarm clock
he nicknames Timebomb. His favourite hobby
is winding it up and just letting go;
letting history run its course
with a backhanded twist

of course.

It's all down to timing, he claims.
All down to timing.

Junk-food for Jaws

With dollars stamped all over you.
Shekels shackling you. Ballots buggered
and bent and bound for Barack, what are
the chances you'll avoid the daggers in
Sharm el' Shark?

One man's meat.
Everyman's poison.
It took a breeze the size of a cyclone
playing Fats Waller to the drone of Greensleeves
to stir you from your feed, US delinquent. Are you

ready for your fully-grown state? 'Cause they've had it
with the pubescent-parrot act, your stubborn, feet-
stamping, sulky, wobbly-throwing, stick-to-your-guns
brigade and its door-slamming antics. Though, not even
you could see through these closed doors. Superman.

The time to draw daffs on tanks is over. You've left off
too many petals and we're not going to sit on the fence
anymore whilst you miss the point. Again. And again. Promises
have lost their meaning. Action is irreversible. So go in peace.
Not up for negotiation.

Gadaffi Duck and the looniest of Looney Tunes

They'd like you to believe
this is just another simple lesson
in altruism. But then again
they'd like you to believe
a lot of things. They tell you

packs of stories of shrunken,
poisoned dwarves fed on protein
supplements; they dress painstakingly

in dark-dust-grey top hats
and baggy pin-striped suits,
too short in the leg to take you
where you want to go. They pass
mildew-rimmed housing facilities.
Beneath railway bridges

unnoticed. They

take pills and scream their tonsils out
like Liza Minnelli in *Cabaret*, fungal
hallucinations breeding gout
off the high-life. Their predecessors
no more original. No less brutal.
Brutality is a subjective habit,

don't you know?

They swig down malignance
with the shady remnants
of their morning Coco-Pops-milk.
It deletes their memory.

Miraculously.
The scale of their ambition
depends on how savagely
they're allowed to deal
with unnamed,
over-armed
despots.

They don't like to let on
that this can be achieved
single-handedly; that they
don't need the paltry opinions
of their bumbling war cabinets.
They prefer to head for the forests,
crouch down around the campfire
chanting spells, telling bedtime tales
of heroics and barbarics and how
they saved democracy

once upon a time. They horde

stuffed camel heads and flog them
as precious collector's items
at some later date. They keep
a few back as a token of nostalgia.
No hard feelings. The camel heads
have fewer fleas

since they were detached
from their necks. 'And anyway,'
comes the bottom line, 'if you
won't stuff your own folk, we will.'
A whisper follows: 'there's no room
for tribal politics here, dearest. Either
you massacre your own people
or we'll do it. That's the pro of democracy:
we give you that choice. Cost not an issue –

military bonuses cover anything from
enemy earlobes to a whole set of fingernails,
authentic copies bound for immediate sale
on EBay – fingertips inclusive as part of
a full complimentary manicure pack. Our boys

in green take pretty pictures of their holiday
highlights so those cheap, irreplaceable thrills
don't have to join the ranks of the ephemeral.
Remember: the most important part about
mass-killing is bragging about it. Insurgency

rocks and rolls but always swings to one side;
the side our boys like to take pot-shots at
in the name of target practice, all art
for art's sake – don't you know?'
How aesthetic can you get?

Butt of the Joke

What did you think the mad bastard would do with those rifles
you sold him? Make Polos out of the Wailing Wall? And maybe
you're thinking, well someone had to sell them to him. But let's face it:

they didn't –

Friends are divided up into desirable and unacceptable, inexcusable
and executable. So who do we insult next year? Whose regime,
culture, identity shall we tamper with? Convert. Whose democracy
shall we manipulate, monopolise, turn into a souvenir? Decimate.

You're on the lookout for genetic birth defects too. Orphans are ideal
when your plague spreads. Less costly than importing rats
and guinea pigs. Even on the sly.

Though war's the filthiest, most malignant rat of them all. And really,
let's be honest,

you have no place *civilising* others
when you haven't so much as started

to civilise yourselves.

For your own good

We want rules without getting into semantics.
We want black and white, shoot and ceasefire;
we want to sabotage and dope up and then
go cold turkey on the whole goddamn lot.

No, don't get into semantics, whatever you do:
modern democracies are going to eat, shit
and murder wherever they like. Anyway.
Having freedom is about blocking everyone else's.

Yes, you keep the wars out of our memory: you bury them
behind the British Broadcasting Craporation, you use
heavy-duty bleach and delete what was there;
you sandpaper the truth, leave the shell smooth and
shiny – as chaste as a baby's birthday suit. You coat
the hood of the planet with glue and iron filings. You
attach hundred-weight magnets and let history do the rest.

But you don't leave your marks. You walk without shadows
and white-iced footprints tack the path from idiocy to greater,
more obtuse acts of idiocy. Never to be naked. Alone. Never
to be liberal. Again. Except when it comes down to babysitting

foreign dollars:

yes, sex in the city, and watch how the banks all coo
at the adorable infant parading through Cheapside
on the one and only black steed that could pass
for pantomime; the powers-that-be who duck and
cringe and stutter at yet another dagger of disrepute.

You run amok, and far from the motherland
with those long, fancy strides. You mothball lies,
truly handsome, insincere, invisible
to the human eye. But we've seen,

you see. We've heard how you repackage terror and treason
on dummy-bomb-runs, shield the offending article
between baby transmitter and paedophilic papers
the pope lost his grip on: there's treason and reason
you cannot distinguish. There's a plug to pull
on Whitehall wollies and an even bigger one
in Washington, where the truth is left to bathe
in a typhus-tub only the FBI may breathe.

Hey ho, honeytraps abound it seems:
a heady adhesive now jumps the gaps
where honey used to muffle peace – Congress,
in the meanwhile, so unaccountably

accountable

when we ask: do you have ambitions
for freedom? You talk of human wrongs
not rights. You talk of secrets stacked up
to the ceiling in order of stolen consequence,
the terrine of life and sentence you prefer
not to eat in eight, even pieces? You prefer
to reserve judgement on the matter and
prioritise bedtime over war crime. You

answer questions with more questions
you're likely to dribble over in sassy
Picasso patterns. Blue Period. Red period.
You get stumped by the traffic lights in three
shades of electric green and accidentally dilute
civil liberties. The CIA has promised to be
selectively colour-blind. Forever.

On a roll

You seem to be on a roll. So,
(whilst you're at it) why not take out
Tunisia, Morocco, Syria, Egypt, Yemen,
Bahrain, civilised Saudi Arabia,

The Ukraine?

Why not take out Uganda, Rwanda,
Zimbabwe, Cuba, Venezuela,
The Ivory Coast? Why not take on
the whole damn planet (except, well,
the obvious…) whilst you're at it? Why not

invite them to high tea at No.10, form a club
for Democratic Despots and drizzle a little
diesel oil in the beverage of their choosing;
replace their scones with SCUDS and jam
with the bloods of their own freedom-fighting
millions? Hypocrisy is just so hip, darling! The
killer-coalition runs full-moons around liberty.

A Cable-Car Named (White) House-Fire

It's out.
He's in.
Finally.

Pastel-eyed
short man
dust-flicking
pink-wearing
devil-worshiping
baby-blond
bum-blistered
buggering
bastard.

And now he's no longer a he.

It's what they'd always wanted.
Anyway. All leaks in moderation
so long as they don't exit
through the rear end.

Top-secret mother tongue
dives her way into a den
of defence dispatches
to unpick all hoodwinking,
deluding, bamboozling
gold-shredded, like-minded displays
of public deception. Conception.
Correction. *But it's the way you tell'em.*
Truth is torture to democracies:

Stand down. Shut up.
Now all locked-up
for want of cloned integrity.
What would you do if…

How much public right is right?
How many lies spell *truth* in hieroglyphics?
Do you need a calculator to work out
the sum of democracy and dictatorship?
Since when does the word rape
carry more weight than the word fire?
The server is there to serve – not salivate.

Who said Military Intelligence
was intelligent? Who said communication
should be limited to old news, untruths
and trivia? How would you classify *tour of duty*?
What would you do if…

Tank

A compass ring of pebbles awakens you,
the sly repetition of a long-overheated rainfall.
They tickle you to laughter, make you shudder
and roll until a ramp of flesh dissolves beneath
your tread. And then there is silence

and just a fistful of sun beating you up

from the inside out, a few more heaped
on the death-toll that you cannot see.
Just hear. The cacophony of sniper
and self-love. From a six year-old's jab
at *let's pretend* to copping off on Capitol
Hill. Blame it all on ejaculation, Honey.

Those pebbles are just fabulous for foreplay.

Short Back and Sides

They've tried trimming
and snipping and snapping
and binning. They've been
cropping and mowing
and pruning and shaving.
They've botched it, shearing
and tearing, hacking off
and lopping off, burning
and brewing and stewing
the lot. And the hairdo
doesn't suit society's
naturally chubby cheeks,
its substantially double,
even triple chin and rosebud-
round jowls. The razor blade
has trashed its safety catch,
slit into vein and vena cava
with less than a care, slashed at
arteries with artillery not built
for this side of the Black Sea;
hoping, just hoping for natural
hair loss. But breeding the one-
way seed of alopecia.

Ironing out Iran

Like a lava of commandments
set down in invisible ink, casting
in stone

the felonious rules of bestiality
that fail to trace beyond the
thought,

their creation: nothing but Houdini-
style loyalties and an overload
of surprise sirens

shaking hands with a notch
of space between; long obedient
details

carved into a syncopated spine
with half-wits choosing the gaps
according to gossip and level of

gain.

Finger-mouse

He hadn't meant to be put on trial like that.

He said, they were of a different opinion:

They tickled each of the remaining five pigs
of his right hand before snapping and carving
in reverse order.

They stopped at two and a half;

enough to make writing difficult, female
satisfaction – the job of other men. Not for
the likes of him.

They said, it was because they'd caught him
having sex

in a tree.

He said, they weren't blessed with imagination.
He said, they didn't care much for his films either

even those made with seven and a half digits.

He said, he was glad they'd left his thumbs,
for want of something to twiddle whilst awaiting
his asylum papers.

He said, he had no intention of letting the other
seven and a half leave the UK again.

He said, the word homesickness meant something
completely different to him.

Night Raid

Tip-toeing downstairs
with the validation of stars
to give away your game,
your trick-or-treating crossfire
and likely scars,

more conspired, than inspired.
You come with impure intentions,
commands from twelve thousand
miles away and counting. Each
blast is the seed to another hackle.
Each hackle is another knife

in the dark, a roadside mine,
a woman cloaked and raped
beneath, an oxygen mask
to a towering inferno,

a recycled fever of eyes
and teeth; a halting, retraction,
cancellation of penitence. It's
the cowardly paradox that hides
behind the shield of night. It sings
and whistles before silence: say
goodnight. Say goodbye. Hush,

hush,

hush.

Pips

'Truth never damages a cause that is just.'
Mohandas Ghandi

The Face of Revolution

It's not Facebook but faces
that drive the revolution.

No.10 – through the eyes of a ten year old

Behind number 10
was evil he said.
And looking 'round and about
I could see by their heads

that they thought so too.

Death is planned in fine detail
beyond that charred door.
He said: all they care for
is killing. Not the young. Nor the poor.
What's left for us
when the world is no more,
when funding for students
is cut to the floor,
and computers have stolen
those jobs from before
and we're sick of our leaders
who lie to the core;
who save up those billions
for weapons and war,
bombard land after land
by breaking the law,
shoot naïve civilians
for oil and gold ore,
Iran and Iraq
and Afghanistan sore?

Yes, the planet is bleeding
on death-painted shores,
whilst the poet's hand peels
to retell the gore,
to issue the truth
bloody and raw,
to set the world straight,
to settle the score.
For you, poets, are the future:
so go bang down that door
with your pens and your minds
you have the power to draw
all the poison that lines
the political paw.

And you can't go back
once you've seen through them all:
prime minister's lies,
society's fall.

And you can't go back
once they've gnawed at your head
because there's evil behind No.10
he said.

A Daisy Chain called History

It was the moment I realised
the daisy chain was made of paper;
that questions were flames
and memory a fag-lighter:

it was the time I asked
why did we even go there – with
souvenir in hand and enough blood
to make the virginal White House blush.

Doesn't take long to tread everywhere:
the world can be yours
poised on the sly side of a needle.
Intervention. Interference.

Same difference. Tell me:
what do you want with their guns,
then their people, culture, religion,
language, land, history, loves, hates;

silenced personalities
trimmed into cornflower blue cloths,
then white, then sealed and mummified. Your job?
Our job? At what point did you consider

Kabul to be profitable, a population hanging
behind glass cabinets amongst an archive
of stuffed reindeer. Twenty years hence.
Archaeology never dies, unlike its trophies. Say,

what do you remember?

The cool, sterile ash falling and spreading
and freezing its impotence in your back yard?
And still you try to jack off, throw call and devil
into the same pit when you're time was up

before you started. You've asked men
to die some more and they just say yes please
because they're young and jobless
and have no chance of raising £9000

without losing extremities
and hell, that pension sounds good.
You and your catalogue of lies and murder:
you chart their comings and goings,

you plaster their destinies
across billboards and TV screens
before they've seen it;
an echo of every other place

they've stamped their feet in
whilst only their voices are silenced,
bungled by outright contradiction:
terror on their front porch.

But do you really care?
From now until the next election
it's only you ejaculating on the planet,
not a Kleenex in sight. Instead

every secret is torn between rounds of Chinese whispers
and waterboard-aquatics:
privatising death just makes it all
that little bit more personal

from one daisy to another.

Debris

What war is there to win?
What morality is there to learn?
What is there left to cite or flee
or burn when there's nothing
and no one to check at check-
points; when all the rot has

rotten?

What is seen

So much could be written
before the first line:

toy soldiers strutting the patch with a medley
of stale super-weapons, their panzer-proud-chests
puffed out in pathological rows
to greet the extent of adversity
they were apparently conceived for;

plateau upon plateau of dysfunctional clout
creates an isle of expunged credibility,
smug thug smirks
and a fistful of rockets
most would rather do without.

Beyond the fencing cribs, babushka types
of every physical age carry beads and crosses
with Mary memorabilia stuck to their prayer books
like family album offcuts –

as if she's really going to help.

How would it be to sit down at the table again
and share food? To put down the crosses
and Warhol replications of a woman
they've never known,

invite philandering rebels
and lax flash Catholics
with their fascist sympathies

and scratch beneath the surface?

I'm all right, Jack

They do not concern us.

We have lawyers and rapists
and misogynists with poly-filler
in hand: there is no leak too big.
There is no kidney too expensive

in Serbia.

So, seasons greetings! Let's shake on it.
Organs just love capitalism.

And anyway, we have compulsory castration
and sleep deprivation on our side. We hide the
unborn billions in treasure troves. We treat
their parents to mass graves. We most like
to lounge beyond the horizon, sanguine and
reckless whenever you close your eyes.

Because they do not concern us.

We fuck the electorate; we laugh in its face
and saw off its head and watch it breed
a thousand Medusas who will never consent.
And still we laugh.

We take all we can get, wrap it up
in gold-shredded Christmas paper
and call it good will. That year

there were torturers and paedophiles
who popped out of the box. Followed
in quick succession by the coalition:
stepped up the rush from fact to fiction
munched up the youth and its right to
tuition; the nude and the starved, no
immediate distinction. And next will be
skin
or muscle,
bone and blood,
the clinics and libraries we'll drown
in the flood, lapped up for dinner with EMA
and green pus, 'cause their future's not ours
and they don't concern us.

Uniform Transparency

If it came down to

colour-coded dialogues,
propaganda still singing
with its heart

half-hanging out, numb down one side,
and struggling to commit to the cause,

there'd be a unicolour rainbow hovering
over the backyard, bombardment

after bombardment, each and every

separatist

equally flammable,
puncturing equally well

and vacuum-pack-stacked
to the skyline
in symmetrical
Emmental slabs,

before they even considered
singing their own praises.

Joker

You bolt the door with those lying, seething
benchmarks of diplomacy – and throw away
the key. A fair trial is a moderate, mediocre one.
Just is merely a linguistic technicality.

Lacquer the latch with silicon. Keep those leaks
from seeping out; keep the outside world
from coming in with its realities, its meddling sores
and invasive actualities. Keep the inside world

from bleating out atrocities, buggeries, torture,
threats and secrecies. But keep looting the authorities
for access. Keep philandering with the truth: avoid
all credible contraceptives and make as many

truth-babies as you can. With men. With women.
With the screen; your nosey neighbour glued to his living
room curtain, your long-lost pen-pal who has a strong
aversion to Facebook, your Labrador's last Kennel

Club trainer, schoolteacher, postman, ex-lovers,
Twitter pimps. 'Cause the leak doesn't sleep,
unlike the lie, which descends to a state where
it practically dies. Dormant. Deceptively so.

Inbreeding its demons. Aborting its crimes.

A fairer (skinned) Constitution –
à la Peste Blonde

They'll be arrested
for picking up rubbish
before you know it:

'hey you sir, why are you
worshipping our roadsides,
crowning curb and terrace

but not curbing your mechanical
motion in any particular way, shape
or form? Tell us: why are you

here, bending and stretching
in our streets, bending and
stretching in our minds, our

foretold legislative prejudices
that even boast a place
in our fragile framework

where you do not belong? Where
you are not welcome. So go
take your aerobic antics else-

where, 'cause we don't want you
or your big-wide-world ideas,
your tinting of our great white-

sharkness, your polluting of our
ballet-fine floral language with
those hefty guttural expulsions

we only phonate following food-
poisoning. You have no place
in our eco-system, no right to

laver in our laundrettes, to breed
your multiple mobs of Maghrebins
on our torn Terre Française, who'll

in turn plash around in our piscines
and drown in the depths of our
discriminations, those of our well-

trained offspring, screaming 'liar,
racist, criminal, illegal, inhuman.'
All falling on double-deaf, triple-

Tripoli-waxed ears the UN, EU
Courts of Human Rights aren't
about to clear. So take your cloths

and scarves and herds of Social-
Security-sapping stock; take your
falafel and Arab rabble, your
prayer books and mats; take your

ethnic prance, your davening
indoctrinating trance away. Away.
Not in La France.

Not in la France.

Geneva Conventionalism

When it's a toss-up between
your minaret and mine, a cone
or a cross or a moon that hacks into a sky
of unlimited fears,

our unlimited fears:

When it means a plebiscite
turning into a fascist site 'cause we're all so twee
and conservative and can't see past the flashing lights
and even flashier dollars of St. Moritz…

'cause that kind of foreigner's okay.
In our minds.
In our constitution:

the kind of guest who stays for a week,
maybe two at a push, with a wrench
at the old purse-strings;

who stays for the status,
for the exclusivity of it all,
for a four minute downhill rush,

and speeding about as far
in the opposite direction
of those blazing minarets
as possible. Because

what it boils down to is:
a prayer call cannot drown out
the yodelééeeeeeeeeeeooooooooooooooooooo.

Silent Tourettes

If it were possible
to turn down the volume,
turn off the speakers,
invert the plastic sheath
that goes bang whenever
air is blown in and out –

If that bang moved in, in,
in and took its poise
between belly and gut,
took comfort in the echo
of the interior when
everywhere else signed

incommunicado:

out of order
out of office;

I just don't want to bloody speak to you.

Who would care? Who gives a fart
about the indoor channel: words blurted out

Tommy-gun-style that cannot console themselves with
pen or paper, a third-hand ear that hears what it wants
to, its cries full of **Hhh**onest **h**ates hovering like bored
incendiaries when there is no smoke screen

and no heavy-duty fire door
and the extinguisher's well past
its sell-by-date?

Tribe

It's not ok

to divide up belief

the way you section landmasses
in line with oil and gold
and human capital reserves.

I wonder who said it was –

slicing up sun-dried tribes
in thirds and eighths
and jagged, misfit puzzle-pieces
with the blunt side of your scalpel.

There are awkward snaps and cracks
where invisible forts and borders
were said to be; livid façades
of unhealed, malformed bone. You

sawed through house and school
with no thought for their contents.
Main thing: redrafting your regional
paper-traces, those shady indelible inks

that mark minds more than Google maps
in how they bleed and stain their intentions
entirely without cause,

utterly ill-informed

as if doodling
in the dark.

Rheumatic Rebellion

Rebellion with a comma, full stop and question mark
all in one. Rebellion sheds tears – sometimes crocodile
ones – cries and barks, but cannot bite. Rebellion needs
dentures to impersonate the snap of the beast he dreams
of becoming. Rebellion shares sentiments he is not aware
of, dazzled by the limelight. And though he is part-sheep
by nature, his voice carries, hoping for novelty, hoping
to be heard by those who are not sheep, who are not
brutal; who are not an apparition of the last hideous

incarnation which dared to name itself government:
recurring, multiplying, blurring,
maligned with stolen interest.

It's not *one more push*
but one hundred hard-labour heaves.
It's not the head of the snake that's poisonous
but the whole slimy bastard: the whole damn
nest crawling alive with the same like-minded
gang of septic hypnotists.

So power to the people! The ones you don't hear
beyond thirty-three years of desert-tread tyranny,
with their muted aspirations and limited, ill-crafted
aims. Because the BBC doesn't go there; doesn't
hear those peoples packed down in neat, treated
pieces between shingle dune and mountain hovel,
the way colonies best like to be kept.

Even one's own.

Free and law-abiding.

We are not oppressive.

That must be stressed.

Dictatorship is what happens
to other nations. And anyway,
it is illegal to think otherwise.

So power to a people who grind grain with stone,
lug water on parted scalps: the sheen of illiterate
voices grows matt and old too quickly to spell change
on withered shoulders. Rebellion loiters all too often,

too arthritic to go anywhere
without a Zimmer frame.

Ha(i)ting

They should meat-cleave them
clean off, coat them in smelted
yellow metals 'til firm and crisp
enough for Christmas trees

and the likes. They should
line the streets of Port-au-Prince
with the famish of Catholic orthodoxy,
sardonic candles boasting troops

of hand-standing stalactites;
frisk and waggle to one-time
ragtime wonders – round the
rape camps and far, far from

refu-g-spots.

How to make humans illegal

I

There's something akin
to Europhobia

behind him;

a dull, off-tone clank
of times past and left
half-mast, those last
marching droves storm-trooping
hammer and sickle in hand, their heap

upon heap

of contradiction
passed from woman
to man to man, filling
the child's fragile skies
with trended red parades
and fascist cries, conflicting lies

of the people's republic.

Everybody equal. Everybody equally
fear-infected, foe-focused. Everybody
equally Europhobic, splaying a double-
hand of double-sided cards, playing
the game as if winning were the only

possible outcome;

probability no more
than an arduous
mathematical fart

aimed at making your schooldays
unnecessarily complicated,
your report card:
unnecessarily
shit.

II

But there they are: the fear-infected;

fighting dogs and warriors who box
and bear-bait and hunt humans
like wild boar hoards. For fun.

Don't you just love the value of life –

delving in and out amongst an enclave
of citrus illegitimates; the skin
and bitter under-flesh

something you peel back
with no remorse? Merely
self-replenishing hunger.
An urge to harm not heal

with ill-wills
and sick hearts
that have forgotten
how not

to hurt.

From a Treehouse

From here, we can see the proles below:

They occupy a department store
they've never once before visited,
one cordon bleu chocolate cube
costing the sum of a full-blown
scoff down the local kebab house.
How to quantify? How to gain
a true sense of proportion when
the next course is caviar?

From here, we can see platoons
of Primark hooligans and Top Shop
slobs, the big society we prefer
to class as small fry can be halved
and halved again: we learned a lot
about fractions

at Eton and Westminster. Playing politics
with a weighted dice; we've painted
the roulette wheel raging scarlet
before taking it on a spin to Libya
and back. Though had we known,
we could have saved on the paint,
used human haemoglobin instead,

tar everything with the same rancid
brush: from privatisation to militarization
to mobilisation to superfluous burial
procedures. All the while, from here,

we can see the public sector flaunting
its beer belly; it could do with losing
a few pounds, a few undergraduates,
disabled claimants, community schools
and sixth form candidates. So we hoist
up its trousers to lederhosen-length,
slice off thigh-high hunks of well-
produced oomph with a generous
slap of the hand. And stab at the

heart. Though every hothead has
his day, standing between trooper
and union, a mismanaged middle-
man with so little to say. Whilst
it all comes down to: do you have

the right name? The right face,
colour and breeding? 'Cause vee
have vays of making *old school*
ze new school, diminished degree
programmes down to a matter
of luck. Not judgement.

Crime on Commission

Falling crime? The more the merrier!
While smaller bait goes bust:

the only business that simply
loves recessions. And wardens
love the profits that go with them

even more

in NY and DC
and canny California.

So don't kid yourself that house protection
and heightened police watch are flattering
your taxes with their ground zero tolerance.
Let's face it: banging up anyone even mildly
suspicious

or not

is going to bring home the bacon. Because

somewhere,

deep-down in those so-called *State* penitentiaries,
fingering the millions, it's not bacon,
but a whopping great suckling.

For Embolism

It hadn't seemed particularly unusual
until he explained the mog bore the title
of embolism,

and probably became an embolism,
shacked up for posterity
on the twenty-sixth floor
with his manic-depressive Goth of an owner
and a neighbourhood of pit-bulls – though

I suppose

there wasn't anything particularly unusual
about that: the pit bulls having mauled each other
and half of the juvenile population of the estate
were allegedly all born-again vegetarians
receiving regular blood transfusions and psychotherapy
care of Jobseekers' Allowance.

Moss Side had never seen such a fall in benefits claims.

The government celebrated.
The government started breeding pit bulls
as part of its back-to-work-or-die scheme.
With a bit of luck they'd shift the debt by 2014,
be in the black
with enough spare cash
for ministerial pocket money and a £10 HMV voucher
for every A&E department, as a show of goodwill.

The suture business had never been so good,
the average waiting time now up to 5hr 19 min,
and that was Monday morning.

For Embolism, this was not such good news:
the Goth, for fear of losing his puss to the pit bulls,
never let him stray beyond the grid of the balcony,
sunlight barred at each and every slit in the stonework,
'til the mog was forced to raid the bathroom cabinet
for anti-depressants,

a permanent supply of Kitty-Kat on tap
along with homo sapien mood swings
as black as his fur arrangement
being about all he had to look forward to.

Until the day he overdosed. On Kitty-Kat.
Contracted a vicious strain of BSC
and committed Hara-kiri on the corner railing.
Not surprisingly the embolism vanished,
as did all the pit-bulls who dined at his expense.
The government mourned.

Illegal Illness

It's official: the stats have shrunk.
It'll be illegal to be sick by 2020.
Disease has been cut. So don't
develop ME, rheumatism or any
strain of mental imbalance
or you'll be pawning breadsticks
for psychiatry sessions.

Don't catch STDs or smoke yourself
to infertility. Don't have an accident
on your front porch without a fully
comprehensive insurance policy:
there'll be no beds to death-rattle in,
no emergency staff at hand to yank
gadgets out of children's noses.

Don't bank on anything other than
this one minute detail: that sickness
will be cut when there is no longer
a service for it. The league tables
will see to that. Just watch how
cancer dribbles off the NHS menu,
how hip replacements halve to a halt.

There'll be no future docs with nous;
just the stupid, rich ones who can
foot the bill and bribe their way into
the medicine cabinet with a sharp
wrench at daddy's little finger. So
don't get sick any time soon. There's
a time and a place. But it's not here.

A Recipe for Resistance

Take 400 grams of marginalisation,
300 grams of unemployment
and an equal measure
of unequal opportunities.

Tip in half a litre of racial abuse,
systematic discrimination and sexual
harassment. Add a generous helping
of social media granules, three large
pinches of hybrid slang and a dozen
drops of concentrated adolescent
fervour. Knead together well with
a limitless portion of stalwart
conviction, irrevocable insults
and a ballooning sense
of stiff-necked injustice.

Roll out into an oasis of oval oblivion.

Sprinkle superstar heroics and a medley
of martyr romantics, now grown on
home turf. No rising agent required.

Bake in oil-fired stone ovens, preheated over centuries.
Forget to check and forget to turn. And wait. Just wait
for those alarm bells to start ringing.

Inevitably.

All that toasting and roasting,
singeing and searing, charcoaled
from burning. You

never thought to use the timer;
thought this pudding would tend
to its own perfection. But then again,

you'd rather make a desert
than a dessert: turn up the heat
and turn your back, and pretend
you had nothing to do with its creation.

You put your hands in the air
at the choice of ingredients.
You say you never bought them:

they took their own trolley and bus-ride
home, stripped and peeled and
grated themselves. These are
imposters, you say;
mutant invaders

not fit for your sauce.

And with that, you mix two heaped
tablespoons of mistrust with double
that of disrespect. You stir in a mug
of moral high ground and ten shots
of corruption. You beat rigorously,
trying to prevent lumps from forming,
the alien residues of denied identity
routinely removed. Routinely dolloped
on top of the garbage dump, in time
with a stolen sense of belonging.

Until you realise you've used
the wrong flour – and this is
neither the time nor place
to be dabbling in gastro.

Vocal Accords

Since when did energy take flight?
Since when did drive jet off
into the sunset?

Where are the whoops and wails
and charges of emotion? The solidary
shriek of belief? The sirens of conviction?

Since when did the worthwhile
lose its value: crowd members
countable on two sets of hands, if

you allowed time enough? What
was the point in importing the word
revolution, if it rings so off-key and

piteously
on ears tuned so well to apathy?
Revolution in costume: it goes

to the ball all dolled down
in hiking boots and jumpsuits
and vacuum flasks of over-stewed

black tea. It means well-meant ideas
but goes about its business with a sickly,
obliging, confused smile around its chops:

the ruling liberal oligarchs are going to
march right over in routine stampedes.
All consequential actions have been

erased. I sit amongst Eisenhower's
circle of confidants. The guard
on the other side of the railing

has developed a nervous twitch
directly opposite, the half-cocked
rifle commanding his grip

appears to poise with me in mind;
my presence, my obliviousness
to his.

His Felix the Cat act quickens,
unnerved by my proximity
and serene, unarmed distance,

my silence and written verbosity.
My opinion. Or is it the rifle manning
his grip which scares him more?

Juice

'We delight in the beauty of the butterfly,
but rarely admit the changes it has
gone through to achieve that beauty.'
Maya Angelou

In the Cupboard

Just let it be over.

We've run out of cats and dogs
and donkeys to eat. Had we

known, we'd have bred them
more enthusiastically. Never
imagined they'd be sacrificed
to a less than lesser god.

It seems

there was greater nutritional value
in the French Revolution.

We're eating grass again:

the grasses and leaves
that have been trampled
and pissed on in exodus;

dried and moistened
and dried more times than
any leaf should have to endure,
than any human should have to

digest.

Though we don't digest.
Of course.

While pistols are on the table
but no bread.

How Social loses sight of Care

Black baby, white baby,
yellow, pink, blue, lilac,
green polka-dotted baby;
an eternity of hysterical
difference sets you apart
and confirms your similarity

match after match. And
the shortage is a lie:
high politics comes in
at every opportunity
with dud-sounding
footprints and a chalice

of misunderstanding.

Too many seats

around the boardroom table
from LEA to local minister
to worn-down, semi-manic-
depressive social worker
to teacher, carer and cop.

And though nothing is resolved
overrepresentation tops the bill
when it comes down to political
point-scoring. A job well done.

More people. More mayhem.
More eclectic indecision.
Another unfinished case.
Another unstarted life.

The Merry-go-round goes round

What are you laughing at?

You have landslides and homicides
and suicides and pesticides and
infanticides coming out of your
backside

and still you shake like a cackling lamb –

You have a generation
on your front porch
and it's pining for knowledge
waving its skyline of opinion
in your fake, foibled face.

But you don't listen for the whispers.
You don't even notice the whistle
warnings between each failed,
monotonous, life-mauling fart.

I say YOU, what are you laughing at?

You have *COWARD* scrawled across your features
in vast, slanting fonts you get wound up in
because YOU laid the chairs out
and every single one of them
has a whoopee cushion called student
on it

psyched-up and hungry – and it
will bite you in the bum
fart and all.

In your back garden, you shave back
the shrubs, saw down the lawn, carve
robin and hedgehog and squirrel
clean out of the picture. You lay down
poison on the plants you will eat
next year (I hope you puke).

Though you have forgotten the weeds,
how they twist and turn, how they outsmart
plant and parasite; how they outsmart you

growing out and down and up, across,
wider, wider, dodging this and that
until finally fly:

tall, gangly, bumptious hieroglyphics
bridging the gap between fossil and fire.
So what are you laughing at

Mr I-have-everything-including-an-Eton-
education; including our education
scrunched up in the palm of your hand?
Because one day when you're old and sick
and fucked up to the hilt with untested drugs
and untested doctors, just remember
who said 'knock, knock' first.

Waste Disposal

Where is the will, imagination, thought, instinct,
self-imposition that gets you to a better place,
a higher plain? What have onlooker's seen
but savage and stupid, binge-like broken instincts,
toxins with no quick-fix antidote, freak-show-style contestants

cooped up in grim-rimmed chicken grids for homes,
their bladed cages promising sharper, steelier freedoms
beyond and stab at the sleekest glint of self-improvement.
Inevitability is government policy at its most austere, MPs
playing bow and arrow from the glistening turrets of Shitehall.

Social mobility is segregating buses and schoolrooms
and city centres; it's being granted permission to breathe,
to smell the weed-wrangled breath of your neighbour
on the other side of the wall: his rising damp, your rising damp:
in the soup with asthmatic, nicotine-hungry kids

who are kicked in the head before they know
what disadvantaged is.

Apocalyptic Shroud

Antiseptic wipes the wound
but not the zit with the interminably
irrepressible pus and his pandemic
poison-bearers. Tank up and bear down,
inject with bile and boils and the ripped,
torn, dead bit picked out of society
like Prometheus' liver, pawned and
tattered like a daily duty, as if a deity's
hand had the final say and didn't really
care much for the creation side of things.

He builds his house out of ready-lit matchsticks,
peels back the ashen hatch to reveal
a tinderbox of strays society still isn't
ready for. They become the all-round
compost

that smokes and grows in the wrong places,
in the wrong direction; they pierce like poison-
dipped darts, the flawless landscape which
turns sick and brown to putrid rotting smut
shades, gnawing down and round in
circumventing worm spirals, through volcanic
plate and urn, through generation and age
and amoebic reproduction, through sound
and light signals, through instinctual birth
and destruction. Down, down, porcelain
banjos. Bang! Survival, but no evolution
sitting at their table.

Hotspot at Chilcot

No one can remember
The internet curiously experienced a blip.
The telephone lines had been snipped.
The VCR was turned off.
The Dictaphone was turned off

… the record.

The webcam was turned off.
Bony Tear's ears were turned off.
Though truth be told, the PM
was turned on.

Stumped

They chip first from the foot up,
grate toenails with blunt cheese knives
down to a gangrenously raw knob of
knuckle. But they let their hair grow.

Leave the lot untreated, weeping
septic carnivals of false pride
like ill-judged incontinence. Are you

under 25, vibrant, optimistic, got talent
and feel genetically bound for success?
Well, you won't be for long. Their reputation
is amputation

unless of course you're a city whiz-kid
flexing your FT pecs, forever flavour
of the month. Foreseeably

plucking all the live petals off
the petunias, tearing up the roots,
pruning back the saplings, watching stem
and leaf tumble and turn to excrement. They

use a pesticide called T.A.X. but harvest
too soon and bleed the earth dry. Some say
it's child abuse planting land mines at a time

where they make snacks out of secondary
schools, hospitals, librarian pools,
no quotas asked. Then come back
for second helpings. How common

is the Common Agricultural Policy?

Slapping Stick

Bring back those corporal junkies,
the hand and whip and lick about
the ear, and undone children's rights.
Let the cane come back to class or
at least let teachers shake the bastards
by the shoulder like their parents

never did

without jade and lilac child abuse sirens
drowning out those of the riot police.

Bring back marching double-time in
schoolyards twice a day. Bring back
bucket-loads of lines and let those
reams wallpaper the larynx of Whitehall.

Bring back polished pumps and ironed
underwear and long white-ribbed socks
strung up to knee-knuckle height like
good Catholic mites. Bring back prison
for the underage and parental indiscretion.
Blame underachievement on the young
and unemployment on the incompetent.
The swines don't want to learn anyway.

Who let them graze in the Cabinet?

What we swallow

I

I watched a building melt to the ground
in time to The Thin Ice

from the comfort of my sofa,

its outer glass garments
drizzling from wick to ramekin
like unwanted advent accessories.

Since when did this become
standard teatime viewing –

Pink Floyd brewing
or rather stewing
in the background

marginally off the boil
and turned
from the exertion,

unsure

how to calibrate.

II

I am even less sure.

He leaves sinewy stains
about the inner rim, the beaker
flaunting its ill-carved mindset;
a chlorinated, off-key Watusi
of bad salty waters

lost in screening

to eggshell-fine slithers
of kettle-lining.

There are buildings still melting
with The Thin Ice long since
turned to a puddle

when the lurking,
deep-sea-diving
tea debris

has finally resorted
to snorkel and goggles, open

to the elements. Exposed
to a lighter insight.
No holding breath
and shutting eyes
and pretending
not to see

when the on-button
is off-ed.

Sublanders

When suspicion overtakes sensitivity
and subtle sympathies, 'cause you
wouldn't want to be there yourself
and despot Lord Mayors peel off
their fake rubber mantels quick as
moulting hyenas reared up on haunches
high and paws spread wide, and claiming
'*I didn't do it*.'

When plasma becomes the number one
political keyword, followed in close succession
by Adidas trainers, and all else holds no interest
or comprehension because nothing more than
a screen and pair of shoelaces – brand shoe-
laces – ties the population together to call itself
culture.

When that culture tells lies and melts or bleeds,
until eventually it evaporates to the feed of a
dripping tap, the brave expectant youth stands
open-mouthed beneath, gasping darling, gasping,
just waiting for those drips.

Or Air pumps.
Or Blackberries.
Or anything else that costs
but a night in the slammer.
'A kick up the rump' says my mother,
'that should do it. A nice fat kick up
the proverbial rear end.'

Photographic Playground

She droops,
eyelids photo-snapping her sporadic days
as grandmother like she did last week,
clutching at familiarity
before a makeshift den of savages
who still favour games of wood and rope;
who Tarzan-yodel across the digital planet
in search of a mate. Conquer. Own.

Each ride is a continent of the world,
another land to parcel up
done and dusted;

another custom to learn
and tongue to tie: nothing
anticipation can prepare you for.

They arrange themselves high. Or hidden.
Stretched and crouched and arched
over their circus like trapeze artist

wannabes; every tunnel and tomb
bends an ear where the giants cannot go.
Pebble on pebble. Electrified mosaic
of stone. Or glass. Smash. Quick. Time to grow up.
Every kid wants to play referee for the winning side,
finger a symphony of sea-life in the sand
and call it a masterpiece.

Henry Moore becomes a knot of architects
all building their own castles.

I ride the tunnel inside.
For that split-second I am not
myself. Falling every strip down the slide
from myself. Far from the gangs who stand
triangled to the climbing wall in slick prisms
of authority. They know what they want.
They harmonise the patch between screech
and song, kissed to a whisper as the sun
dims the cold hide of the slide's
perfectly mirrored limbs;

a crescendo of pleasure
springs from the whistling kettle my grandmother
always forgot to remove from the hob of a morning.
Her memory a roundabout. Going nowhere.
Yet still she wants another spin.
Same, same. As it was before.

I drive the cockpit of a photograph
she calls the past, the mosaic all white
in her day. The playground never changes.
Only the kids. Their folks. The words they exchange.
'How do you play?' they ask. But playground framed in time.
Hers and mine. Yours.

Playground still breathing. Still not beat
by Gameboy and PS three hundred and wotsit.
Though maybe hibernating, dozing goddess aglow
in the six o'clock sundown: reclining spiders set alight
the pert corners of your smile.
They outline the immensity

of your features. Serene sculpture.
I don't know what you're thinking.
I can only guess.

Open barrel – closed door

Rewinding

It wasn't until they turned around again
that they noticed someone had cunningly
taken the Great

out of Britain; a loose sense of Tsunami
that had wreaked havoc far and wide,
and done its business where none

was required. No retract. No firm tact.
Trees boasting genital wart protrusions
all over the scene like the final unwritten

chapter of The Joy of Sex. Without the
joy bit. Jailbirds, curfews, criminal advisory
panels poncing all over the shop, picking

and mixing cocktails of founded and
unfounded cliché. Not really heading for
anything average, relatively balanced.

Relevant. MPs who've never set foot
outside the private sector lock horns
on street corners, tussling over a matter

of letters in pelican and pedestrian
crossing, the lights and stripes that order
their playground puppets, as if Punch

and Judy were anything but a pantomime.
Move over and watch those Ford Escorts
charge, baby! Put your money where your

mouth is. (The one in your face) Scream,
sizzle, display human characteristics that
don't show signs of faked constipation

the way you foul up and fade away,
mashed voicelessly into commoner's
tarmac, freshly rolled gravel bits steamed

into your arsehole. (The one at your rear
end) There's no stopping you when you
let rip – TNT untested. British Safety

Standards have dropped the British bit.

Mr. Fixit

They go in for a kidney transplant
and come out with cancer.

They go in for a blood transfusion
and leave with HIV.

They go in for breast implants
and exit one ovary down.

The NHS goes in for its budget review
and emerges wheel-chair-bound.

And this year's med students go in
full of conviction, but leave quietly,

inconspicuously, surreptitiously
through the private corridor.

Free-climber

Where have you been?
We couldn't stand
how you turned your head
and looked the other way
as if forward were no longer

a direction.

Forward has become
a procession of undolled-up
ultimatums, accidental sanctions,
boastful annexations. Forward

has come to mean freefall:
abseil like a pan-Olympian
in search of his kudos;

summit after summit of tracing
trapped satellites and informal
burials, care of all participating
3rd party tour operators. They

run a bring-your-own rope
and chain policy – allegedly for
hygiene reasons. Separatist
flags free of charge; free of
postage and packaging
and on your own head

if the tanks don't get there first.

New Dawn

New dawn.

But how permanent does revolution have to be
to keep the dawn new and shiny
and squeaky clean?

There can be no end of protest
while there're tears without teargas,
bullets fired

but not from guns.

Because there're lies from any president
whether he stands down
or up
to the side
with a pirouette and entrechat
or not at all.

There is fear and scepticism,
thug and thespian. There's
a dawn every day

and there is nothing new about

that: fresh out-of-a-five-pack
of M&S underpants
over old unwashed crotch.

Military crotch

dragged through mud and blood
and shit, uncertain of station
amidst a regime of Russian dolls:

the same illegitimacy lurking beneath
the same illusion of new doll, new dawn.
Chop them up. Chop them off
and still they grow back
ten times more virginal
with their coy, painted smiles
and perfectly,
identically
listed fingers:

and they are all Mubarak
until the final one has gone.

Tahrir – Before the Tambourines

In the stretch from tyranny
there were lists, long and sly,
alligators squeezing out the remnants
of back-splashed teargas, their offspring
tendering batons

and a wrench of rubber bullets
casually raining down in bastard
sound mutinies, mapping out
the swamps of oceanic quicksand:
the challenge of Saracen-plump
assault tanks; of torn, swept-up,
pissed-on squares, of poorly
equipped clash-crowds

with nothing but freedom-speak
on their side, nudging their pride.

They lick the wound of the rule
of law. They aim and fire by
street-strike, unhinge the backbone
of Tahrir, vertebrae for vertebrae
in their million-dollar, million-man
marches. They kick the badest

and blackest of bad-arse back-teeth,
a salad of real-life pirates whipping
the brittle with a flat lacquered hand.

It glides over state sceptics with only
solvent credibility, a spill of constitutional
die-hards and sectarian bloods flow
cocktail-smart like a fast-forwarded

pilgrimage. Artillery rounds select

death in thin symmetrical zigzags:
armoured carriers have eaten out
the still panting offal of revolution
amidst a rich mix of lithium-kissed
fibs; the potbelly of propaganda
prefers its favourite pre-dinner binge
out of the newspaper. Silence

becomes a veil of dehumanisation,
a sword of guilt, a volley of ammunition
and suspended killings interspersed
between stale election sweats:

interim Cabinets with interim love
potions but no remedy. Just bile.
Offshoots. Revisited. Same again.

Lunchtime Loving in EC2

There was no more than coincidence to it,
finding love amid lunchtime's frantic, fodder-
hunting mob, love set fast among thick white
bricks in bankers' belt, all tarred with the same
static-grey brush, all dulled by the verminal hue
of their pin-sharp pin-stripes. It wasn't planned
that I'd sit there among them, Pied Piper to a congress
of frigid wizards drawn to the trough. They roll past
in their mobile cages, a sushi meal set to double-time,

head down, snout first. A cavern of seasickness
storms my head: I'm forced to lower my eyes.
I ground myself. I think of a better way, a finer
cast or setting. I consider self-sufficiency,
a caravan and a handful of land. The
verminal suits become vermin, rather
than humans pretending to be. The speed
around me normalises. There are two tunnels,
two train tracks, two circuits of independent,

adjacently flowing blood streams that cannot
intertwine. On both sides of the rectangular patch
we stare: your pleading, jealous, trapped gaze
just seems to make you walk all the quicker.
But you'd hate my side. You wouldn't know
what to do with it; where to start and what time
to finish. It wouldn't mean anything for you to land
by chance in front of a street sign reading Love Lane
because you'd forget it was there. And I like the fact

that I won't.

Trading Places

Friend, let me tear open your gut. Let me start
with a quick prod, then a rip, so that my fingers
get inside and chance their way between the folds
of your conscience like vaselined seals, rich to richer

on the fat of your impoverishment.

Friend, we make imbeciles of your scientists;
we make devils of our own. You are an inspiration to us
and we're going to run you over, run your market,
even your women: just to show you

how appreciative we are.

Bet you never thought you'd be selling t-shirts
at £1 a piece and below at all markets
and major boutiques, that you'd be extinguished
as quick as fire in a chippie;

that we, the others, in our billion-seater jet
could be the oil that once fried your Catholic cod
every Friday, the flames that spread so far
and lit all your fags simultaneously.

Bet you never thought we'd become the fat black smoke
that hangs in both left and right lung, the fruit
of your constitution, every last cigarette
you have puffed away at and now banned.

Though I am the smoke.
The fat, black smoke.
And I am still here, getting fatter and fatter.
And I will choke you.

Getting Ahead

I've been there before
but rarely enter: that place
where my fears breed, shrink,
multiply, die, reincarnate

simultaneously. Feet falling,

face failing. Can't face
failing and falling.

I am not a control freak.

But the unknown is a rope
around my submissive left foot,
whilst the right straggles, yanks,
procrastinates, unable to follow
a sky dressed as the ground,
pave, benches, pigeon stool.
There's no end to surprise
and her henchwomen

as I tumble through time
toes pointed full stretch
out front

in the hope
the future
will become
the present
sooner,

before I realise
it isn't mine yet.